Tatsuo Miyajima

Big Time

Tatsuo Miyajima
Big Time

Organized by Michael Auping

Modern Art Museum of Fort Worth
in association with the Hayward Gallery, London

Hayward Gallery

sbc

Beck's is pleased to sponsor Tatsuo Miyajima's exhibition *Big Time* at the Hayward Gallery. Beck's association with the artist dates back to the 1995 Beck's/Artangel collaboration during which Miyajima's *Running Time* was housed at the Queen's House, Greenwich. It is exciting that we can now help to achieve this realisation of *Running Time*, and other works, in a gallery setting. The Hayward Gallery also holds particular significance for Beck's, as the venue of one of our earliest large-scale sponsorships, the Gilbert and George exhibition, in 1987. This was successfully followed by Richard Long's *Walking in Circles* four years later. These two events occupy a special place in Beck's history as limited edition Beck's bottle labels were produced to commemorate both exhibitions. We are very happy that Tatsuo Miyajima has also agreed to create a new label for the Beck's bottle. We hope that a great many people will take this opportunity to see the first large-scale gallery showing of Tatsuo Miyajima's work at the Hayward Gallery.

Tatsuo Miyajima: Big Time was organized by the Modern Art Museum of Fort Worth in association with Sun & Star 1996. The Founding Sponsors for Sun & Star 1996 were EDS and Hitachi, Ltd. This exhibition was funded in part by Alliance Development Company, Fuji Electric and Pier 1 Imports, Inc., through their support of Sun & Star 1996.

Contents

Foreword

When Sun & Star 1996 came to us over a year ago with their plans to celebrate Japanese culture in Fort Worth and Dallas we were delighted. As a museum dedicated to the presentation of contemporary art from around the world, we welcomed the opportunity to participate and to bring to Fort Worth and Dallas new art forms that reflect an aspect of vanguard thinking in Japan.

Michael Auping, the museum's Chief Curator, has chosen to devote our galleries to one of Japan's most dynamic young artists. Over the past decade, Tatsuo Miyajima has attracted considerable international attention with his provocative installations of electronic digital counters. Continuing the Japanese tradition of exploring time and space as a form of artistic subject matter, Miyajima's mesmerizing technologies forge a poignant union of the ancient and the new.

I would like to thank Michael for his devotion to this complex project and elegant catalogue. We would also like to acknowledge the support of Sun & Star 1996, which helped finance this ambitious presentation.

It has been a pleasure to welcome Tatsuo Miyajima to Fort Worth, and we appreciate the work he has put into our installation. The spectacular results speak for themselves.

Marla Price
Director

Hayward Gallery Foreword

The Hayward Gallery is pleased to present the first major exhibition in Britain of work by Tatsuo Miyajima, one of Japan's foremost young artists.

Miyajima's installation, *Running Time*, garnered much critical acclaim and public attention in its spectacular presentation at the Queen's House in Greenwich as an Artangel commission in 1995. We are delighted that audiences here will have the opportunity to see a new version of *Running Time*, adapted specifically for the Hayward Gallery, along with five major installations from the past seven years, seen here for the first time.

We are immensely grateful to Marla Price, Director, and Michael Auping, Chief Curator, of the Modern Art Museum of Fort Worth, who initiated and originally organised *Big Time* and who have generously given their fullest support to the Hayward showing. We are also grateful to Claudio Silvestrin, for his thoughtful architectural design, and to Lorcan O'Neill and Jim Cohan of the Anthony d'Offay Gallery, London, for their advice and assistance. We are particularly indebted to all the lenders who kindly agreed to extend the loan of works from their collections.

We are also most grateful to Beck's for their support of the Hayward Gallery showing and delighted that the Miyajima exhibition here has provided another opportunity to continue our relationship with them.

Not least, our profound thanks go to Tatsuo Miyajima, for the care, knowledge and enthusiasm he has brought to the preparation and presentation of *Big Time* at the Hayward Gallery.

Susan Ferleger Brades
Director

Susan May
Exhibition Organiser

Preface and Acknowledgements

Following his graduation from Tokyo National University of Fine Arts and Music in 1984 and completing post-graduate studies from there in 1986, Tatsuo Miyajima gained international recognition almost immediately. His inclusion in the Aperto section of the prestigious Venice Biennale in 1988 announced a powerful and innovative new voice from Japan. Since that time, Miyajima has had one-person exhibitions at the National Gallery of Canada, the Kunsthalle Zurich and The Queen's House, Greenwich, London. This present exhibition is the artist's first one-person museum exhibition in the United States.

In the course of organizing this exhibition, I have had the help of numerous colleagues. The assistance of Jim Cohan and Sadie Coles of the Anthony d'Offay Gallery, London and Roland Augustine and Lawrence Luhring of the Luhring Augustine Gallery, New York has been crucial. They have provided photographs and research materials, and both galleries have lent important works to the exhibition. I would also like to acknowledge Jessica and Robert Baron, Janet de Botton, Dr. Donald Fraser, Collection Goetz, Munich, Germany, Sarah-Ann and Werner H. Kramarsky, Sissy and Siegfried Loch, and Marc and Livia Straus, who have generously lent works from their private collections. A large and technically complex project like this one demands the attention of virtually every member of the museum's staff, and I am very grateful to my co-workers at the Modern Art Museum of Fort Worth. Among them, I must especially thank Marla Price, Director, for her unwavering encouragement. I would also like to acknowledge the exceptional efforts of Susan Colegrove, Administrative Assistant, Tony Wright, Head, Design and Installation, and Andrea Karnes, Registrar for their work on the catalogue, installation and shipping arrangements respectively.

This catalogue has been a collaborative effort between the artist, Peter Willberg and myself. On behalf of Tatsuo and myself, I'd like to thank Peter Willberg for synthesizing a number of ideas into an elegant and straightforward publication. While accompanying our exhibition in Fort Worth, this catalogue also is designed to have a life of its own. The color plates illustrate works in the exhibition, as well as other important works

11

produced by the artist over the past 10 years. The quotations accompanying many of the images were chosen by the artist. The artwork is not designed to illustrate the quote nor is the quote an explanation of the artwork. Juxtaposed they suggest a third statement relating to Miyajima's preoccupation with time.

Sun & Star 1996, an ambitious, Texas-based festival celebrating the contemporary and historical achievements of Japanese culture, has been a critical partner on this project from the outset. Their financial support has been crucial in the organization of the exhibition and this publication. Along with the distinguished Board of Sun & Star 1996, I would like to acknowledge their able staff, particularly Susan Barnes, Debra Skriba and Anna McFarland. We are also grateful to Alliance Development Company, Fuji Electric and Pier 1 Imports, Inc. for their sponsorship of this project.

Finally, I owe my largest thanks to Tatsuo Miyajima, whose intelligence, hard work and good humor have been an inspiration throughout the making of this exhibition. We are, indeed, proud to present his work in Fort Worth.

M.A.

Theater of Time
Michael Auping

Those familiar with Tatsuo Miyajima's art will generally tell you that time is the subject of his work, when in fact it is more appropriate to say that time is the object of his work, if one can think of time as an object of awareness. We – who attempt to define, understand and measure time – are the subject of the artist's relentless counting. It is undoubtedly for this reason that Miyajima's stark, conceptually-based art strikes a surprisingly personal and immediate chord of recognition with so many viewers. In many ways, Miyajima's art symbolizes humanity's innate ambition to understand what may be the heart of reality. Time is so fundamental to our psyche, indeed, our very sense of existence, that it eludes us. Its definition remains a mystery; its shape and measurement a scientific and spiritual challenge. In the final paragraph of his popular book *A Brief History of Time*, Stephen Hawking imagines a "complete theory" of time that could be broadly understood by everyone, not simply a few specialists. "Then we shall all," Hawking speculates, "philosophers, scientists, and just ordinary people, be able to take part in the discussion of the question of why it is that we and the universe exist. If we find the answer to that, it would be the ultimate triumph of human reason – for then we would know the mind of God."[1]

Like Hawking, Miyajima sees our understanding of time as fundamental to a basic definition of religion and spirituality. The artist, who began studying Buddhist philosophy when he was age 23, refers to Buddhism simply as "a religion about time."[2] Miyajima's continuously changing numerical images address the enormous challenge of visualizing the complexity of a vast universe – as defined by both Buddhist philosophy and modern physics – where the individual is a tiny but significant unit within an immense incomprehensible whole.

There is a street-smart literalness to Miyajima's electronics, however, that belies their spiritual and philosophical underpinnings. He does not imagine himself a priest, shaman or guru. Like any artist, he is essentially an inventor, using images to construct a particular view of reality, and his interest in concepts of time emerged gradually and unpretentiously. Born in middle-class east Tokyo, the artist originally aspired to be a carpenter

1 Stephen W. Hawking, *A Brief History of Time: From the Big Bang to Black Holes* (New York: Bantam Books, 1988) p.175.
2 Unless otherwise indicated, all quotes are from interviews between the author and the artist, September 12–14, 1995.

like his father.
school initiate
Tokyo Nationa
accepted, he v
vation, a temp
and measuren
and about diff
basic, not clea
As a stud
artist initially e
of these perfo
and the cause
In 1981 in Toky
audio, videota
his action. Thi
impact of the
Founded in 19
graphic traditi
contemporary
Jackson Pollo
multimedia er
Happenings ir
formances als
1970s by such
Nauman, mar
sizing process
enacted in tin
"An effective
"You have to t
or too short.
when to be m
of any perforr
At the er
tions to these
a particular c

was not always accessible for the audience. I only performed a work once. I never repeated a performance. If you missed it, you would never see it again. That was important, but a weakness, not accessible enough." Accessibility remains a key issue for Miyajima, not only from the standpoint of creating an art of some permanence, but also in the artist's attraction to materials that are associated with popular culture, materials that look familiar rather than "aesthetic." So, according to Miyajima, "I made an object."

Between late 1984 and 1987, what Miyajima made were a series of electronic, Rube Goldberg-like devices. During this period, the artist searched electronic scrap yards for cast-off technologies (old televisions, transistor radios, etc.) that could be pieced and wired together to form a new entity with an improvised electronic nervous system. These mixed media constructions – involving sound, image and various combinations of motion – were, in effect, performing objects. Miyajima's admiration for Jean Tinguely's rambunctious machines of the 1950s and 1960s was embodied in a new generation of electronic and digital forms. Eventually,

15

NA. AR. (Voice), 1981, Tokyo.

Miyajima brought these performing devices together into family groups. *It of the Future*, 1986, for example, consists of a room-sized environment of a series of machines, each electronically connected to the other. A viewer entering the room activates an optoeletronic switch which sets the machines in motion, triggering a chain reaction of random movements and images: a neon light flashes in one area, as a picture is projected in another; as one motor begins to move, a second machine may be suddenly stilled, etc. These "events" were programmed so that no sequence of images or actions would be repeated. Such a work indulged Miyajima's need for something that approached sculptural permanence, yet allowed him to explore elements of motion, reaction and duration. Unlike many technological works that project a clinical and abstract relationship to human presence, Miyajima's constructions evoke empathy for human processes, often mirroring them. The viewer communicates with the object, as the reaction of the machine is a reaction to the viewer's be-havior, and in a sense metaphoric of the variable character of human personality.

16

It of the Future, 1986. Scrap, machine, monitor TV, video, light, IC, diode.
Installation, 275 $1/2$ × 137 $3/4$ × 78 $3/4$ inches.

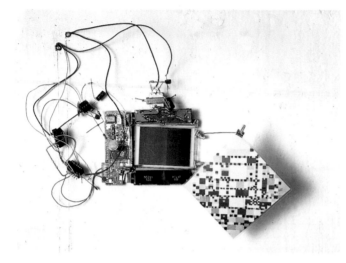

While *It of the Future* has characteristics which embody Miyajima's appreciation of Tinguely's kinetic machines of the 1960s, it was in fact an important stage in the artist's search to evoke "a specifically Asian or Buddhist viewpoint rather than a European one." *It of the Future* emerged in a period when Miyajima was forging a philosophy in which technologies could be used to express the humanistic as well as spiritual qualities of Far Eastern art and religion. In constructing *It of the Future*, Miyajima examined some of the prominent characteristics of his work to that point and reflected on the qualities of Buddhist philosophy that most attracted him, looking for points of convergence. The artist eventually identified three basic themes that would guide his future work: 1) keep changing; 2) continue forever; 3) connect with everything. These concepts remain the guiding maxims of Miyajima's art.

In 1987, the artist had an exhibition at Gallery Lunami in Tokyo, for which he created three works, each of which reflected at least one of the three concepts. Among these was a work referring to the search for pure or transcendental abstraction, and specifically the paintings of Piet

17

It Goes on Changing (Copy of Work by Piet Mondrian), 1987.
Liquid crystal TV, IC, electric wire, photo. 7 7/8 × 7 1/8 × 2 inches.

Mondrian. The reference to this revered pioneer of the abstract sublime is both an homage and a sly critique. *It Goes on Changing* (Copy of Work by Piet Mondrian), 1987 consists of a tiny liquid crystal television set juxtaposed to an illustration of Mondrian's famous painting *Victory Boogie Woogie* of 1944. Electronic signals are sent randomly to the small television monitor, producing a varied series of colors and shapes that appear as abstract "pictures." While Mondrian's image is static, Miyajima's is constantly in motion. Miyajima acknowledges Mondrian as making art about the infinite and the spiritual. "I think he thinks about God, infinity and the void. So, he also made an art as time. It is great work, absolutely perfect art as static, no movement, not changing. I want to make things that are permanent but also change. Infinity, like time itself, is constantly changing." Such works reflect the first of Miyajima's three basic concepts: keep changing.

Clock for 300 Thousand Years, 1987, also created for that exhibition, represents the artist's half-mocking attempt to suggest the relentless character of the infinite. Counting time in units of $\frac{1}{10}$ seconds, Miyajima's digital clock counts to 9,999,999,999,999 – 9 trillion 999 billion seconds, approximately 300 thousand years from now. By creating an artwork that has a finite lifetime, but one that will not be complete until long after we are gone, Miyajima has embraced an increment of time that seems distant enough relative to a normal life span to suggest the horizonless character of time itself, as well as begging the question of what time means beyond human existence, and to what degree time exists without human awareness. *Clock for 300 Thousand Years* thus symbolizes the concept "continue forever."

A third work, *Nachi Falls*, 1987, completed the artist's philosophical triad. Titled after one of the most famous scenic spots in Japan, *Nachi Falls* addresses a single subject as depicted in different periods of time and media. Read from top to bottom, the work consists of a copy of a late 13th century painting of Nachi Falls by an unknown Japanese artist, to a video monitor showing a stream of water flowing across the screen, to a cassette recorder emitting the sounds of Nachi Falls. Near the floor, Miyajima has placed a copy of a painting of birds and flowers by an early 16th century Japanese artist, Motonobu Kano. Below that, a video monitor submerged in a tank of water, broadcasts "live" scenes from the actual basin of Nachi

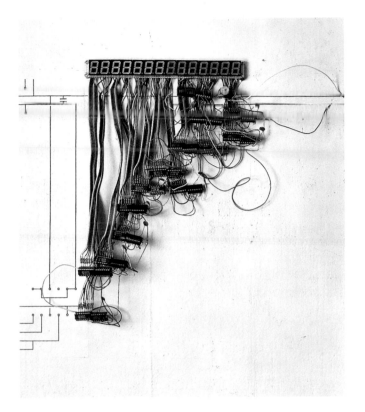

Falls. Miyajima describes the entire image as a "waterfall of time," in which one image connects many points of time together, representing the artist's third theme: "connect with everything."

Although pleased with the philosophical coherence of this 1987 exhibition, Miyajima began to search for an object, material or situation that could elucidate all three of his basic concepts in one image or statement. To this end, Miyajima made his first counting device – or as he refers to it, "gadget" – at the end of 1987: it was a small light emitting diode (LED) that counts from one to nine repeatedly. This generic technological device symbolizes for Miyajima the most basic visualization of the passage of time, and has become one of the fundamental building blocks of his art. Over the years, the artist has pieced increasing numbers of these units together to create evermore complex statements. Miyajima's employment of the term "gadget" downplays the appearance of spectacle and "special effects" that are often associated with electronic art. The artist describes his gadgets as "simple constructions" made by someone with no special training. Miyajima is not an electrical engineer. Any skills he has acquired have

Clock for 300 Thousand Years, 1987.
L.E.D., IC, electric wire, line tape. 9⁷/₈ × 7¹/₈ × 2 inches.

come from working with various components in a trial and error manner.

In the 1988 work *Sea of Time*, Miyajima strung together 300 separate counting units, operating synchronically but at different speeds. As the artist explains it, "Each machine operates in sync with another machine. As the 'time' counted by one mechanism reaches '99,' a second machine will count '1'; when the next '99' is reached by the first mechanism, the second will count '2,' etc." Thus, *Sea of Time* visualizes hundreds of different "times," all counting within the same visual field, which symbolizes no absolute time but rather a network of individual rhythms. For Miyajima, time is comparable to color in that it is unique and personal for everyone. Miyajima's Buddhist beliefs are also reflected in the circular repetition of counting from one to 99 and returning again to one, suggesting a revolving cycle of time, and the concept of death and rebirth. Zero, which indicates an end, is never used. Miyajima describes *Sea of Time* as depicting "a kind of world or universe. Each counter could be a different person or a different planet. And these counters together make the whole world, the universe." Indeed, one of the metaphoric attributes of these counting machines is their sly humanness. Like the human body, they operate on electrical impulse. The fluid, relentless counting mesmerizes, while certain rhythmic sequences parallel one's own breathing or heartbeat. In combining four of his gadgets together – with the ability to receive and transmit signals to each other – and titling the work *Family*, the artist further stresses the human metaphor. Each gadget is a surrogate human presence; larger groupings can be imagined as families, communities and worlds.

Scattered over the entire floor of a room, *Sea of Time* immerses the viewer in a spatial as well as a temporal experience. Subsequent works such as *Counter Line*, 1989 and *Counter Circle*, 1988 are equally bold in activating the entire space of a room or building. The former consists of a line of LED counters stretching over 15 feet, while the latter coupling of counters forms a large circle. As before, individual counters operate at different speeds, suggesting a seemingly infinite number of ways of dividing and defining time. These shapes also suggest an added symbolic dimension. *Counter Line* refers to time as a linear concept, an orientation that Miyajima sees as being predominantly Western. The circle, which is a sacred shape in Japan, symbolizes Eastern time. *Counter Line* and

Counter Circle can be seen as both an acknowledgement of these attempts to shape time, as well as a critique of them. Rather than using zero, his counters move from one to nine, and then go dark, creating various momentary breaks in the form. After a short time, the counting begins again. Miyajima sees these recurring voids as "a cut into the line" of a preconceived definition of time, an erasure of the shape. Miyajima's point is that time has no shape. Or, conversely, it is all shapes and all directions. Indeed, Miyajima contends that "*Counter Line* and *Counter Circle* are possibly one shape. If we draw a very long line on the surface of the earth we will make a circle finally." Elaborating on his unstructured and non-hierarchical view of time, Miyajima created *Lattice*, a series of x-shaped, diagonally positioned counters mounted on a long wall that depicts time as moving in all directions.

The expansive installation of *Lattice,* 1990 belongs to one of Miyajima's most ambitious concepts, the *133651* series, 1990, out of which a number of subsequent works have emerged. The artist acknowledges that most people will not grasp the *133651* concept initially, due to its overwhelming vastness, both as an idea and a visualization. "Even myself, the creator, can not see its entire picture as it would be an enormous experiment … an experiment to express the whole universe in relationship to the law of causality and connections." *133651* consists of an immense field of various groupings of 10 counters each, and the number of possible connections between these groupings. Basically, the system works in the following way: The *133651* series is composed of many units, each unit containing 10 gadgets or individual counters each, arranged next to each other. Each gadget counts at a different speed. The sending and receiving of "count-up" signals occurs within the group of 10. Specifically, communication takes place between a receiver and a sender in discreet pairs. Thus, a maximum of five counters can be connected to five other counters within each unit. This involves many possible configurations; the total number of possibilities being 133651, hence the title. Each unit, whose total number of possibilities is a multiple of seven, uses a green light for the individual counters. All other configurations use red. These 10 counter units, no configuration of which is ever the same, are the building blocks, as it were, of Miyajima's art works. The number 10 was chosen for each group for mathematical, as well as spiritual reasons. The number 10 represents the human being

23

← *Sea of Time*, 1988. L.E.D., IC, electric wire. Installation, 369 × 263¼ × 2 inches.

or life force in Buddhist philosophy. It also allows the most complex number of relationships between groupings.

Miyajima resists describing the mathematical aspect of his art for fear of losing his audience in the minutia of mathematical progressions. He prefers to think of *133651* in terms of the imaginative and metaphoric possibilities of scale. On a metaphoric level, describing *133651* is similar to trying to elucidate how the atom eventually configures the universe. Logistically, the entire *133651* series could not be practically presented, demanding potentially miles of exhibition space. As a result, Miyajima began to construct it as a series of parts. Indeed, much of the artist's work is conceived in terms of part-to-whole relationships. If time is the ultimate holistic field, then everything Miyajima makes refers to something larger than itself. In essence, the immense *133651* is a model universe, a huge field that exists in the artist's imagination and as a numerical possibility, but that is practically impossible to conceive as an artwork. It is an idea similar to, but a step beyond, *Clock for 300 Thousand Years*, 1987, in that it refers to an ultimate and infinite field of time, while accepting the limitation of only being able to present a part of that field. The work *Region*, 1991, which consists of 49 units of 10 counters each, is also conceived by the artist as a part or "region" of the *133651* concept. As Miyajima puts it, "The sky is an immense image, too big to see as a whole, but if you isolate a small section of sky it is still sky, and refers to something always larger."

Miyajima followed *Region* by building an even larger chunk of the *133651* field. *Counter 3,000*, also of 1991, consists of 300 groups of 10 counters each – the largest number of units the artist has used to date – spread floor to ceiling over four surrounding walls. The viewer is virtually immersed in a galaxy of changing numbers. Unlike earlier works such as *Counter Line*, *Counter Circle*, *Lattice* and *Region*, which were designed in specific configurations, the counting units in *Counter 3,000* were placed on the wall intuitively, without a specific design in mind, emphasizing the idea of randomness and chaos, essential qualities of time. The only other instance where this occurs is in the earlier floor piece *Sea of Time* in 1988. Formally speaking, *Counter 3,000* is an elaboration of *Sea of Time*, but applied to the wall, engaging the entirety of a viewer's peripheral vision. A sea of time has become a universe of time.

Since *Counter 3,000*, Miyajima's work has undergone a number of radical and inventive transformations. Foremost among these is the development of his *U-cars*. Following a series of wall-bound, stationary works, Miyajima explored the possibilities of complicating his images of time further by adding the element of movement in space. "My counters up to this point were fixed to a wall or stationary on the floor. The numbers changed, but the thing, the container, did not. I wanted more change to complicate the situation." Following a year of experimentation and development, Miyajima created a miniature (7½ × 4¾ × 3½ inches), battery-powered car, the body of which supports one of the artist's classic LED counters. Eventually, he made 30 *U-cars* and allowed them to move randomly on a black floor. Programmed with sensors at each end, these miniature bumper cars automatically change direction when coming in contact with another car or wall. The glowing numbers atop each vehicle count from one to nine consecutively and back. The resulting impression is that of a pool of black with changing numbers appearing to float over the floor like numerical fireflies. Ideally, *Running Time* should be seen from above,

Counter Circle, 1988. L.E.D., IC, electric wire. Installation, 118 × 118 × 1¼ inches.

looking down into a dark void (the floor has been painted black or covered with black photographic paper) at a spectacle of changing numbers moving in all directions, gliding silently through darkness.

Miyajima embraced the car not so much to make a satiric statement in regards to Japan's dominance in the field of small car manufacturing, but because of its versatility and ability to maneuver easily in every direction, and thus create a greater sense of randomness and chaos. *U-car* refers to "uncertainty car." Taken at face value, this title is a humorously accurate description of his car's uncertain direction. It is also a reference to the German physicist Werner Heisenberg, the founder of quantum mechanics and his "uncertainty principle," which essentially proposed that any measurement of motion and time involves inaccuracies because of the existence of inevitable variables. Einstein's earlier "theory of relativity" postulated that time and space have no universally fixed measurements and that such measurements depend on the relation of the frame of reference to the object measured. Heisenberg complicated Einstein's solution. According to physicist D. R. Murdoch, "Heisenberg believed that the uncertainty is due to the unavoidable disturbance of the object by the process of measurement. All observation involves an interaction between the object and the instrument of observation."[3] While Einstein sought precision in his ideas regarding space and time, Heisenberg suggested that the best we could expect was an educated guess. As Miyajima sees it, "Heisenberg could live with chaos. It's interesting that Heisenberg's theory comes out of Einstein's theory but mysteriously ends up being against it. It's an irony. I think the *U-cars* have this irony built-in to them. It is an ironic combination of two opposing theories."

Like *133651*, *Running Time* suggests both macro and micro models of reality, from the possibility of atoms and neutrons colliding into each other to a solar system of planets and stars in a constant and restless expansion. The imaginative possibilities of scale consistently intrigue Miyajima as he explores new metaphors for expressing the expansiveness of time and space. In describing his work, the artist seldom refers to its physical qualities but rather its conceptual possibilities. "There are billions of stars in the galaxy, just as each person is made up of billions of cells. So the scale of the person and the universe is similar. We carry around a universe of cells

3 D. R. Murdoch, *Dictionary of Modern Culture*, ed. Justin Wintle (London: ARK Paperbacks, 1984), p. 163.

at the same time we fly through a universe of planets. In Buddhism, one person can represent the universe and the universe is not bigger than one person. Both are immense and very mysterious." In a number of respects, the *U-cars* are an inventive summation, containing key qualities of his earlier works' physical movement (the very early kinetic sculpture); a sense of the multi-directionality and randomness of time (*Lattice*); as well as architectural scale (*Sea of Time* and *Counter 3,000*).

Beyond being a hypnotic and frankly entertaining event of flashing numbers, the *U-car* installations are symbolic of the deeper levels of content that fuel Miyajima's inventions. "I chose the car for two reasons. First, because it moves. Second, because of its relationship to our concept of time, to the idea of time history." Part of Miyajima's investigations involve exploring time from a historical standpoint, and he understands the history of our perception of time as being radically affected by the invention of various transportation devices, specifically the ship, the train, the automobile and the airplane. The various changes in our sense of movement, speed and distance associated with these inventions have obviously had

Detail, *Running Time,* 1994.
L.E.D., IC, motor, battery. Individual U-car, 7^1/$_2$ × 4^3/$_4$ × 3^1/$_2$ inches.

profound effects, initiating the very concept of "time zones." Miyajima has also attached his glowing LED counters to small HO train sets, which move in a specific configuration around a room.

Around the same time that he produced the *U-car* concept, Miyajima created *Spiral Time*, 1992, a series of LED counters which are placed in a spiral configuration around two floor-to-ceiling columns. Here again the artist embraces a symbolic design, a powerful logo that has contained deep meanings over the centuries. The spiral has been used by many cultures as a diagram or scheme for fundamental phenomenon, including the concept of growth and the evolution of the universe. Perhaps most commonly, it has been used as an emblem of cosmic motion, with profound implications regarding existence and time. The Greek god of time, Kronos, was often represented holding a spiral snake with two heads. The spiral image, open to all directions, moving forward and back simultaneously, is also a classic visualization of eternity. The symbol of the double curve in Miyajima's *Spiral Time* expresses the interconnecting of two opposing principles, or the Chinese yin and yang symbol. For Miyajima, the spiral is a fundamental symbol of what his art is about, a succinct emblem of the marriage of form and chaos. One of Miyajima's descriptions of the spiral is "the closest symbol we have of a landscape of time."

The term landscape often surfaces in Miyajima's discussions of time, and in the last few years images of nature and references to time intertwine in fascinating and didactic ways. In the *Time Landscape* series, 1993-94, the artist paints over the surface of 19th-century Asian landscape paintings, except where the template of a number has been placed. Areas of the original paintings – which the artist has purchased from various art and antique dealers – have thus been left unpainted and visible in the form of a number. Fragments of the original image peek out from under Miyajima's painting – a branch of an apple blossom tree, part of a swimming carp, etc. – as memories of another time confused and infused into that of our own. In essence, Miyajima pays homage to traditional scroll painting, and what the artist refers to as "Buddhist space and time," while different times and events are presented within a single narrative. In the broadest sense, *Time Landscape* evokes Miyajima's belief that time is nature in its most profound and pure condition. The artist's recent *Over Economy* series,

1992–93, works on the same principle. Sheets of different national currencies are painted over with acrylic except where the numerical template has been placed: a double pun and reference to the concepts that "time is money" and that time in fact changes money as value.

The artist's most recent work, *Time in Blue*, 1996, reflects Miyajima's continued fascination with electronic flashing numbers, his primary means of effecting – both literally and metaphorically – a degree of "enlightenment" on the constant presence of time. *Time in Blue* consists of a large wall of bright blue LED counters, arranged randomly and counting at different rates. The technology to produce a blue LED has only recently been developed to the point that it would be bright enough for Miyajima's purposes, allowing him to finally create a work he had conceived a number of years ago. Miyajima's fascination with blue can, on the one hand, be traced to his longtime admiration for the great blue canvases of Yves Klein and Barnett Newman. Like his predecessors, Miyajima gravitates to the mystery and symbolism of blue. For Miyajima, "... color has the suggestion of form and image: red is a square, yellow is a triangle, blue is a circle.

29

Time Landscape, 1993.
Gouache on magazine image. 55⁷/₈ × 66⁷/₈ inches.

So blue is like no form. Blue is like chaos." Most poignantly perhaps, blue is the color of the sky. It is not lost on Miyajima, of course, that in looking at the sky, ancient people discovered the first clock.

The development of Miyajima's art has itself been circular, spiraling back on earlier ideas and forms. A year ago, the artist returned to performance, where the element of time originally surfaced in his work. In February of 1995, Miyajima assembled 45 people from different countries in Greenwich, England, the site of Greenwich mean time. Each performer, speaking in his/her native language, counts out loud 9, 8, 7, 6, 5, 4, 3, 2, 1, and then a silence for zero. Miyajima describes it as "… using the human body as a counter gadget. All of the languages speaking together with the audience looking down on them." Like the *U-cars*, the performers are allowed to move freely in a contained space. A similar and ironic quality of systematic randomness pervaded the performance, as the personal cadence of each speaker created a living field of individual rhythm and "times." The larger irony, of course, is that each of Miyajima's performers contradict the very notion of Greenwich mean time.

The nature of time has always intrigued artists and philosophers in the East and the West, but particularly so over the past two decades as we come to the end of a millennium. Andy Warhol's infamous eight-hour film *Empire*, 1964 was not about a famous building in Manhattan, but the raw uneasy experience of the passage of time. Jonathan Borofsky's sculpture *Counting* – which consists of a four-foot stack of 8½ x 11 inch sheets of paper on which the artist has been laboriously handwriting numbers consecutively beginning with one, since 1969 – established time as a kind of personal drawing. Rather than sign his works, Borofsky often simply assigns them the number he has currently reached at the moment of the work's completion.

Miyajima specifically acknowledges the work of On Kawara, who moved permanently from Tokyo to New York in 1965. In 1966, Kawara began his series of *Date Paintings*, which consist of a small canvas containing a meticulously painted image of the date he executed the painting, along with a box containing newspaper clippings from the same day. The artist's "postcard" series involved sending daily postcards to friends with the simple statement of what time he got up that day. A similar series of telegrams were also sent announcing only "I am still alive." On Kawara's public meditations on time and "being" constitute a stark form of existentialism that in Miyajima's art has metamorphosed into a social as well as a cosmic dimension. Miyajima has said, "Time is elemental nature on a cosmic level."

It is often argued that Japan's current avant-garde refutes nature-centered aesthetics so long associated with Japanese art in favor of an ironic commentary on the commercial and technological realities of the urban Japanese environment. Nature and technological progress, so the argument goes, are at loggerheads, with nature the ultimate loser. Miyajima's art, however, disputes the idea that technology is necessarily in opposition to nature, although he is fearful of viewing nature as a fixed image of pastoral beauty. In discussing his electronic devices, the artist points out that "electricity *is* nature," the blood of our electronic world. Typically, the artist describes his intentions in expansively philosophical terms. "It is not about creating a beautiful image or system, it is more about creating an inner spiritual quality in the world. My idea of the future is not a pictorial image but a spiritual concept." Ultimately, Miyajima's art invokes a form of secular humanism. He believes that art is one way of triggering moments of enlightenment and self-fulfillment without recourse to supernaturalism. He particularly acknowledges the influence of the philosopher Daisaku Ikeda, whose lectures and writings reflect a form of Buddhism embodied in a movement known as Soka Gakkai International. Ikeda stresses the need to integrate technology and spirituality toward creating a "global unity of mankind." Miyajima reflects Ikeda's philosophy when he remarks, "I use numbers and technology because they are a world language. They can be a basis for discussion and thinking." In Miyajima's eyes, the theater of time is an ultimate common denominator.

Tramp: Oh, well where do you live?
Gamin: No place – here – there – anywhere.
Tramp: Anywhere? That's near where I live.

David Robinson, *Chaplin: His Life and Art*, 1985

Running Time, 1994. Forty U-cars mounted with L.E.D. counters. Individual U-cars, 7$\frac{1}{2}$ × 4$\frac{3}{4}$ × 3$\frac{1}{2}$ inches each.

In Western Europe, time is expressed as a snake. In East Asia, it is a dragon. On the American continent, it is symbolized by a two-headed serpent, with one head representing life and the other, death.

Marie-Louise von Franz, *TIME – Rhythm and repose*, 1978

Double Spiral, 1992–96. L.E.D., IC, electric wire. Two columns, 120 × 12 inches each.

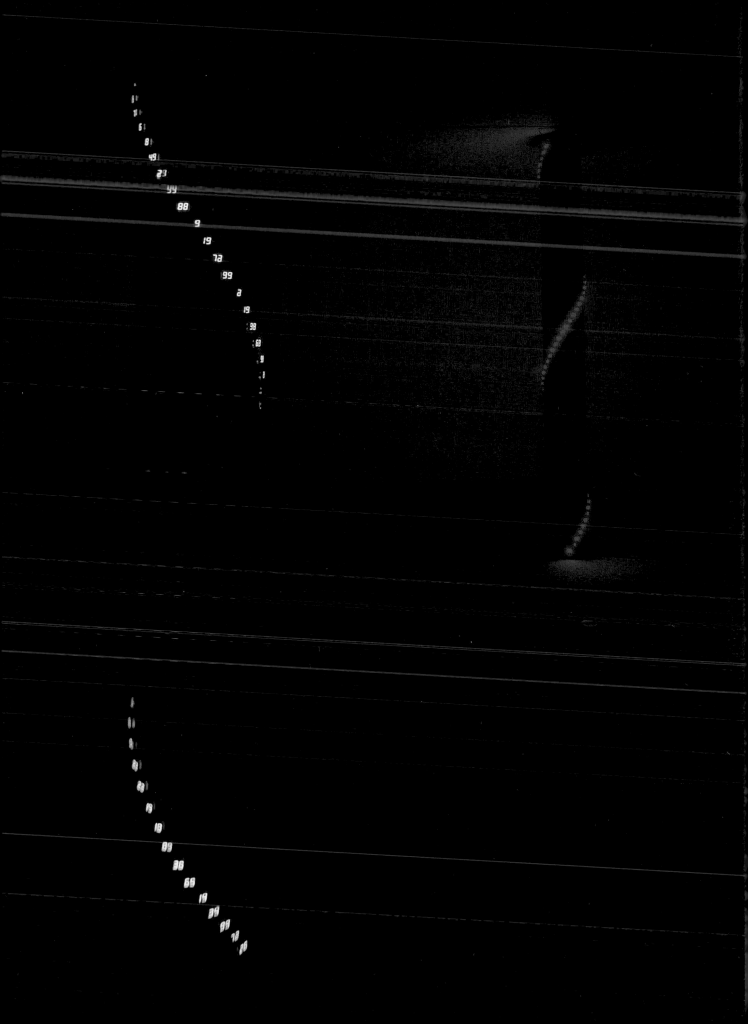

Zwei Dinge erfüllen das Gemüt mit immer neuer
und zunehmender Bewunderung und Ehrfurcht,
je öfter und anhaltender sich das Nachdenken
damit beschäftigt: Der bestirnte Himmel über
mir, und das moralische Gesetz in mir.

Two things fill the mind ever new and increasing
wonder and awe, the more often and the more
seriously reflection concentrates upon them:
the starry heaven above me and the moral law
within me.

Immanuel Kant (1724–1804)

Drawing for Time in Blue No. 29, 1996. Collage, pencil, pen on paper. 60 × 47¼ inches.

People cannot see "time".
They can only see "clocks".

Shuji Terayama, *Kamen Gahou*

Time Go Round, 1996. L.E.D. counters on rotating arms. Dimensions variable.

Time is Money

Benjamin Franklin (1706–1790)

Over Economy, 1992–93. Gouache on Japanese banknotes. 3$\frac{1}{8}$ × 5$\frac{3}{4}$ inches each.

Ikeda: I too think that time and space are concepts created by the human mind and that if we attempt to find out what their true natures are, we are compelled to return to the nature of the greater life force.

Arnold Toynbee and Daisaku Ikeda, 1976

Time Landscape, 1994. Pencil and acrylic on 19th-Century Chinese landscape of Qing Dynasty. 51¼ × 12¼ inches.

4	2	2
6	3	3
2	6	2
3	4	0
7	8	2
2	6	9
9		
7	5	3
2	3	4
1	5	

It is at work everywhere, functioning smoothly
at times, at other times in fits and starts.
It breathes, it heats. It shits and fucks. What
a mistake to have ever said *the* id.

Gilles Deleuze and Felix Guattari, *Anti-Oedipus,* 1984

Sea of Time, 1988. L.E.D., IC, electric wire. Installation, 275 1/2 × 275 1/2 × 2 inches.

All things are in a state of flux

Herakleitos (540–480 BC)

Luna, 1994. L.E.D., IC, electric wire, aluminum panel, plastic case. 394 × 14 × 69 $\frac{1}{2}$ inches.
Installation on exhaust tower, Tokyo.

Einstein: Then truth and beauty have nothing
to do with humans and exist independently.
Tagore: That's right.
Einstein: So, if humans were to cease to exist,
would the Apollo Belvedere cease to be beautiful?
Tagore: Yes.
Einstein: I agree with you concerning beauty,
but when it comes to truth, I can't agree.
Tagore: Why? Is it because truth is realized
through humans?
Einstein: I cannot prove that what I believe
is correct, but this is because of my religious
conviction.

Albert Einstein and Rabindranath Tagore Tetsuhaku-shobo

Revive Time in the River, 1995. L.E.D., IC, electric wire, plastic coating. 4¼ × 1 × 1⅜ inches × 300 pieces.
Installation view in the Urakami River, Nagasaki.

Nous ne pensons pas le temps reel. Mais nous
le vivons, parce que la vie deborde l'intelligence.

We do not think real time. But we live in it,
because life is greater than intelligence.

Henri Bergson, *L'Evolution créatrice*, 1907

Clear Zero, 1995. Performance at Queen's House, Greenwich, London.

Imaginary time may sound like science fiction, but it is a well-defined mathematical concept. It is time measured using what are called imaginary numbers. The use of imaginary time seems essential, in order to formulate Quatum Mechanics, and the Uncertainty Principle properly. It can be thought of as a direction of time, that is at right angles to the ordinary, or real *time* that we experience.

S. W. Hawking, *Black Holes And Baby Universes*, 1990.

Model (100), 1994. L.E.D., IC, electric wire, aluminum panel, aluminum joint (green). 29 1/8 x 29 1/8 x 15 1/2 inches.

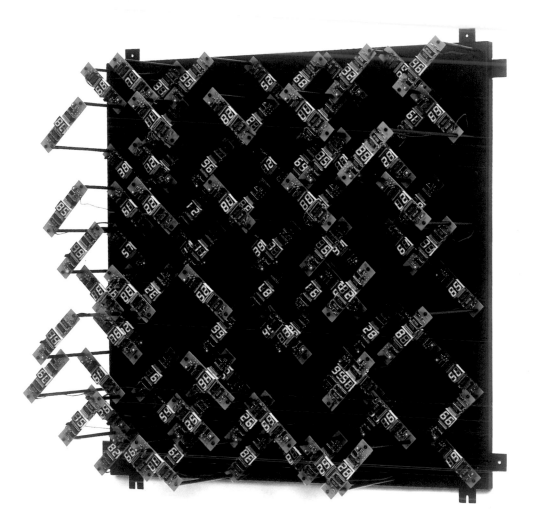

To see a world in a grain of sand
And a heaven in a wild flower,
Hold infinity in the palm of your hand
And eternity in an hour.

William Blake (1757–1827)

Counter 3000, 1991. L.E.D., IC, electric wire, aluminium panel. Installation, 13$\frac{1}{8}$ × 93 feet.

Checklist of the Exhibition

Lattice, 1990
L.E.D., IC, electric wire,
aluminum panel
Dimensions variable
Collection Janet de Botton, London

Lattice, 1990
L.E.D., IC, electric wire,
aluminum panel
Dimensions variable
Collection Marc and Livia Straus

Over Economy, 1992–93 (p. 41)
Twelve drawings in gouache on
American, Canadian, English, French,
German, Italian and Japanese banknotes
$3\frac{1}{8} \times 5\frac{3}{4}$ inches each
Collection Sarah-Ann and Werner H.
Kramarsky

Time Landscape, 1993
Pencil and Chinese ink
on original Japanese painting
$40\frac{1}{4} \times 16$ inches
Private Collection, England

Time Landscape, 1993
Oil on original scroll painting
by Korean artist Shun So
$40\frac{1}{4} \times 16$ inches
Collection Sissy and Siegfried Loch

Time Landscape, 1993
Pencil and acrylic on
19th-Century Korean painting
$39\frac{3}{4} \times 11\frac{3}{4}$ inches
Collection Queensland Art Gallery,
Brisbane, Australia

Running Time, 1994
Forty U-cars mounted with
L.E.D. counters
Individual U-cars, $7\frac{1}{2} \times 4\frac{3}{4} \times 3\frac{1}{2}$ inches
Courtesy Luhring Augustine Gallery,
New York

Time Landscape, 1994
Pencil and acrylic on 19th-Century Chinese
landscape of Qing Dynasty
$52\frac{1}{4} \times 19\frac{1}{4}$ inches
Collection Goetz, Munich, Germany

Time Landscape, 1994 (p. 43)
Pencil and acrylic on 19th-Century Chinese
landscape of Qing Dynasty
$51\frac{1}{4} \times 12\frac{1}{4}$ inches
Collection Jessica and Robert Baron

Big Number, 1996
Wall drawing, painted gold number
to be changed daily
$96\frac{1}{2} \times 48\frac{1}{8}$ inches
Courtesy Anthony d'Offay Gallery, London
and Luhring Augustine Gallery, New York

Double Spiral, 1992–96 (p. 35)
L.E.D., IC, electric wire
Two columns, 120 × 12 inches each
Courtesy Anthony d'Offay Gallery, London
and Luhring Augustine Gallery, New York

Time Go Round, 1996 (p. 39)
L.E.D. counters on rotating arms
Dimensions variable
Courtesy Anthony d'Offay Gallery, London
and Luhring Augustine Gallery, New York

Time in Blue No. 29, 1996
Sixty-one blue L.E.D. counters, IC, electric wire
$175^1/_2$ × 89 × $3^7/_8$ inches
Courtesy Anthony d'Offay Gallery, London
and Luhring Augustine Gallery, New York

Tatsuo Miyajima

1957 Born in Tokyo, Japan

1984 Graduated from Tokyo National University of Fine Arts and Music

1986 Completed postgraduate studies at Tokyo National University of Fine Arts and Music

One-Person Exhibitions

1983 Gallery Paregon, Tokyo. Jun. 13 – 18, 1983.

1986 Maki Gallery, Tokyo. Jan. 6 – 12, 1986.

Akiyama Gallery, Tokyo. Nov. 3 – 22, 1986.

1987 Suntory Art-Box Gallery, Tokyo. Feb. 20 – Mar. 31, 1987.

Lunami Gallery, Tokyo. Dec. 14 – 26, 1987.

1988 Heineken Gallery, Tokyo.

Galleria Vivita, Florence. Oct. 15 – Dec. 10, 1988.

1989 Gallery Takagi, Nagoya, Japan. Mar. 11 – Apr. 28, 1989. Catalogue.

1990 Hiroshima City Museum of Contemporary Art, Japan. *Hiroshima Installation*,
Feb. 10 – Mar. 4, 1990. Catalogue.

Luhring Augustine Gallery, New York. Jun. 2 – 29, 1990.

Gallery Takagi, Nagoya, Japan. Jun. 5 – Jul. 7, 1990.

1991 Museum Het Kruithuis for Contemporary Art, Hertogenbosch, The Netherlands.
Tatsuo Miyajima, Apr. 20 – Jun. 16, 1991. Catalogue.

DAAD Galerie, Berlin. *Tatsuo Miyajima*, Jun. 3 – Jul. 14, 1991. Catalogue.

National Gallery of Canada, Ottawa. *Projects by Artists Series*,
Sep. 12 – Nov. 17, 1991.

Nagoya City Art Museum, Japan. *Region*, Sep. 21 – Nov. 10, 1991. Catalogue.

Galerie Max Hetzler, Cologne. Oct. 11 – Nov. 9, 1991.

Anthony d'Offay Gallery, London. *Region 133651*, Dec. 5, 1991 – Jan. 11, 1992.

1992 Iwaki City Art Museum, Japan. *133651*, Mar. 7 – 29, 1992.

Gallery Takagi, Nagoya, Japan. Nov. 14 – Dec. 26, 1992.

1993 Kunsthalle Zurich, Switzerland. *Running Time*, Jun. 5 – Aug. 8, 1993. Catalogue.

1994 Gallery Takagi, Nagoya, Japan. Apr. 1 – 28, 1994.

Galerie Buchmann, Basel, Switzerland. Sep. 27 – Oct. 19, 1994.

Nasubi Gallery, Tokyo. Dec. 20, 1994 – Jan. 15, 1995.

1995 Luhring Augustine Gallery, New York. *Running Time*, Jan. 7 – Feb. 11, 1995.

Queen's House, Greenwich, London. *Running Time – Clear Zero*,
Feb. 1 – Mar. 5, 1995.

Gallery Takagi, Nagoya, Japan. Sep. 1 – 29, 1995.

Anthony d'Offay Gallery, London. *Drawings and Mirrors*, Sep. 13 – Oct. 14, 1995.

Fondation Cartier pour l'Art Contemporain, Paris. *Tatsuo Miyajima*,
Apr. 12 – May 19, 1996.

Galerie Froment & Putman, Paris. *Tatsuo Miyajima,* Apr. 16   Jun. 1, 1996.

Oakville Galleries, Oakville, Canada. *Tatsuo Miyajima*, Sep. 7 – Nov. 3, 1996.

Selected Group Exhibitions

1983 Kaneko Art G1 Gallery, Tokyo. *Performance Week.*

Plan-B, Tokyo. *Digo once more*

Video Gallery SCAN, Tokyo. *SCAN, Spring Competition.*

1984 Wave Gallery, Tokyo. *Sound Object Exhibition.*

1985 Osaka Prefectural Contemporary Art Center, Japan. *The Hidden Animals in the City.*

1988 Hara Museum of Contemporary Art, Tokyo. *Hara Annual*, Mar. 12 – May 8, 1988.

Venice. *The Venice Biennale, Aperto '88*, Jun. 26 – Sep. 25, 1988.

The Museum of Modern Art, Saitama, Japan. *Movement and Modern Art*,
Oct. 8 – Dec. 11, 1988.

Los Angeles. *East Meets West: Japanese and Italian Art Today*, Dec. 10 – 14, 1988.

1989 Silpakorn University, Thailand. *Japan: A New Generation*, Jan. 23 – Feb. 18, 1989.

Frankfurter Kunstverein and Schirn Kunsthalle, Frankfurt. *Prospect '89*,
Mar. 23 – May 28, 1989.

Hanae Mori Building, Tokyo. *The Seven Artists '89*, Apr. 25 – May 7, 1989. Catalogue.

Musée National d'Art Moderne, Centre Georges Pompidou, Paris. *Magicien de la terre*,
May 14 – Aug. 18, 1989.

Rooseum Center for Contemporary Art, Malmö, Sweden. *What is Contemporary Art?*,
Jun. 2 – Jul. 30, 1989.

Grey Art Gallery & Study Center, New York University; MIT List Visual Arts Center,
Boston; and The Japan Foundation. *Against Nature: Japanese Art in the Eighties.*
Traveled to San Francisco Museum of Modern Art, Jun. 15 – Aug. 6, 1989;
Akron Art Museum, Ohio, Sep. 8 – Nov. 5, 1989; MIT List Visual Arts Center, Boston,
Dec. 9, 1989 – Feb. 11, 1990; Seattle Art Museum, Mar. 22 – May 13,
1990; The Contemporary Arts Center, Cincinnati, Ohio, Jun. 8 – Aug. 10, 1990; Grey
Art Gallery, New York University, Sep. 10 – Oct. 27, 1990; Contemporary Arts Museum,
Houston, Nov. 16, 1990 – Feb. 12, 1991. Catalogue.

The Museum of Modern Art, Toyama, Japan. *Moving Images New, The 4th
Contemporary Art Festival*, Jul. 22 – Aug. 27, 1989.

Museum Van Hedendaagse Kunst Antwerpen, Antwerp, Belgium. *New Tools,
New Images*, Europalia Japan '89, Oct. 1 – Dec. 3, 1989.

Institute of Contemporary Arts, Nagoya, Japan. *ON KAWARA Again and Against –
24 Prominent Works of Japanese Contemporary Art 1966 – 1989*,
Nov. 4 – Dec. 24, 1989.

1990 Third Eye Centre, Glasgow, Scotland and Nicola Jacobs Gallery, London. *Reorienting: Looking East*, Jan. 20 – Mar. 4, 1990. Catalogue.

Contemporary Art Gallery of Art Tower Mito, Japan. *The Game of Manners: Japanese Art in 1990*, Mar. 22 – May 6, 1990.

Sydney. *The 8th Biennale of Sydney – The Readymade Boomerang*, Apr. 11 – Jun. 3, 1990.

Daniel Buchholz, Galerie Gisela Capitain, Tanja Grunert, Galerie Max Hetzler, Jablonka Galerie, Galerie Isabella Kacprzak, Esther Schipper, Monika Spruth Galerie and Galerie Sophia Ungers, Cologne. *The Köln Show*, Apr. 26 – May 26, 1990.

Joensuu Art Museum, Finland. *Worlds–Maailmat 90, International Arts Show*, Jun. 19 – Aug. 31, 1990.

Deste Foundation for Contemporary Art, Athens. *Artificial Nature*, Jun. 20 – Sep. 15, 1990.

Frankfurter Kunstverein, Frankfurt. *Japanische Kunst der 80er Jahre*, Sep. 28 – Nov. 18, 1990. Traveled to Bonner Kunstverein, Bonn; Museum Moderner Kunst, Vienna; Bregenzer Festspiele, Austria.

Deutsches Postmuseum, Frankfurt. *The Disappearance of Distance*, Oct. 2, 1990 – Jan. 13, 1991.

The New Museum of Contemporary Art, New York. *Rhetorical Image*, Dec. 6, 1990 – Jan. 27, 1991.

1991 The Museum of Fine Arts, Gifu, Japan. *Contemporary Arts – The Mind of Japan*, Feb. 16 – Mar. 24, 1991.

Touko Museum of Contemporary Art, Tokyo. *Zones of Love – Contemporary Art from Japan: Touring Australia and New Zealand*, 1991. Traveled to Art Gallery of Western Australia, Perth, Jul. 18 – Sep. 1, 1991; Art Gallery of South Australia, Adelaide, Sep. 20 – Nov. 3, 1991; Waikato Museum of Art and History, Hamilton, New Zealand, Dec. 12, 1991 – Feb. 2, 1992; Dunedin Public Art Gallery, New Zealand, Feb. 27 – Apr. 19, 1992; Museum of Contemporary Art, Sydney, Jun. 3 – Aug. 2, 1992.

The Museum of Modern Art, Saitama, Japan. *Line in Contemporary Art – Destination of Eyes and Hands*.

Mattress Factory, Pittsburgh. *The 51st Carnegie International*, Oct. 19, 1991 – Feb. 15, 1992. Catalogue.

Japanisches Kulturinstitut, Cologne. *Zeitgleich Miyajima/Opalka*, Nov. 16 – Dec. 20, 1991. Catalogue.

Tate Gallery Liverpool; Whitechapel Art Gallery, London; and Malmö
Kunsthalle, Sweden. *A Cabinet of Signs – Contemporary Art from Postmodern Art*,
Dec. 13, 1991 – Feb. 2, 1992.

1992 The Museum of Modern Art, Shiga, Japan. *Shiga Annual '92 – Functions of Language
In Contemporary Art*, Jan. 5 – Feb. 16, 1992.
Chicago Avenue Armory, Chicago. *Art at the Armory: Occupied Territory*,
Sep. 13, 1992 – Jan. 23, 1993.
The Institute of Contemporary Art, Boston. *Performing Objects*,
Dec. 2, 1992 – Feb. 21, 1993.

1993 Fondation Cartier pour l'Art Contemporain, Jouy-en-Josas, France. *Azure*,
May 28 – Sep. 12, 1993.
Taejon Expo, South Korea. *Special Exhibition of Recycling Through Art*,
Aug. 7 – Nov. 7, 1993.
Oita Contemporary Art Exhibition, Japan. *Propose to the Urban Environment –
Impractical* [2], Oct. 9 – Nov. 23, 1993.

1994 Gallery K, Oslo, Norway.
Spiral, Tokyo. *Of the Human Condition: Hope and Despair at the End of the Century*,
Feb. 1 – 20, 1994.
Yokohama Museum of Art, Japan. *Japanese Art After 1945: Scream Against the Sky*,
Feb. 5 – Mar. 30, 1994.
Kukje Gallery, Seoul, South Korea. *Cosmovision*, May 13 – Jun. 10, 1994.
The Museum of Modern Art, Shiga, Japan. *Time in Contemporary Art*,
May 21 – Jul. 17, 1994.
O Museo Temporario, Lisbon. *Multiples Dimensions*,
Jun. 7 – Jul. 30, 1994. Catalogue.
Carre des Arts du Parc Floral de Paris. *Gaze*, Jun. 7 – Aug. 31, 1994.
Sogetsu Kaikan, Tokyo. *Art Against AIDS, Japan*, Sep. 1 – 13, 1994.
Kunsthalle Wien, Vienna. *Jetztzeit*, Sep. 2 – Oct. 23, 1994.
Sezon Museum of Modern Art, Karuizawa, Japan. *Art Today 1994*,
Oct. 8 – Dec. 4, 1994.
Museo Nacional Centro de Arte Reina Sofia, Madrid. *Cocido y Crudo*,
Dec. 14, 1994 – Mar. 6, 1995. Catalogue.

1995 Museum of Contemporary Art, Tokyo. *Art Japan Today*, Mar. 19 – May 21, 1995.   65
Hillside Terrace, Japan. *Field for Intersect*, Apr. 11 – May 7, 1995.

Meguro Museum of Art, Japan. *Japanese Culture: The Fifty Postwar Years*,
Apr. 19 – Jun. 4, 1995.

Louisiana Museum, Humlebaek, Denmark. *Japan Today*,
Jun. 23 – Sep. 24, 1995. Catalogue.

Nagasaki, Tokyo, Japan. *Ripple Across the Water '95*, Sep. 2 – Oct. 1, 1995.

Rochdale Canal, Manchester, England. *Ducks Not on a Pond, Ganders Never Laid a Golden Egg*, Sep. 23 – Oct. 31, 1995.

Istanbul, Turkey. *Istanbul Biennale Orientation*, Nov. 10 – Dec. 10, 1995.

1996 Chiba City Museum of Art, Japan. *Tranquility*, Jan. 4 – Feb. 25, 1996. Catalogue.

The Museum of Modern Art, Wakayama, Japan. *Emits Light, Moves, Makes Noises – Non-Static Art in the 20th Century*, Feb. 24 – Mar. 31, 1996.

Kawaguchi Museum of Contemporary Art, Japan. *Requiem – Koji Enokura and 33 Artists*, Mar. 29 – Apr. 14, 1996.

Selected Bibliography

1989 Mammi, Alessandra. "Tatsuo Miyajima." *Artforum* (New York), Jan. 1989, pp. 125–26.

Koplos, Janet. "Tatsuo Miyajima at Gallery Takagi and Gallery Surge." *Art in America* (New York), Oct. 1989, pp. 225–26.

Baker, Kenneth. "Against Nature: San Francisco MoMA." *Artforum* (New York), Nov. 1989, pp. 159–60.

1990 Lutfy, Carol. "Gaining Face: Japan's Artists Emerge." *ARTnews* (New York), Mar. 1990, pp. 143–47.

Heartney, Eleanor. "Mixed Messages." *Art in America* (New York), Apr. 1990, pp. 213–18.

Brooks, Liz. "Reorienting: Looking East." *Artscribe* (London), May 1990, p. 75.

Brown, Azby. "Tatsuo Miyajima at Luhring Augustine and Gallery Takagi." *Asahi Evening News* (Osaka), Jun. 15, 1990.

Decter, Joshua. "Tatsuo Miyajima." *Arts Magazine* (New York), Oct. 1990, pp. 116–17.

Heartney, Eleanor. "Against Nature: Primal Spirit." *Contemporanea* (New York), Oct. 1990, pp. 76–81.

Larson, Kay. "Made in Japan." *The New Yorker*, Oct. 1, 1990, pp. 63–64.

Brass, Perry. "Word Art at the Aldrich." *Ridgefield Press, Weekend Magazine* (Connecticut), Dec. 5–6, 1990, p. 13.

Faust, Gretchen. "Against Nature: Japanese Art of the '80s." *Arts Magazine* (New York), Dec. 1990, p. 105.

1991 Koplos, Janet. "Dossier: Tokyo, Japan." *Sculpture* (Washington, D.C.), May/Jun. 1991, pp. 24–25.

Gopnik, Adam. "The Art World: Empty Frames." *The New Yorker*, Nov. 25, 1991, pp. 110–20.

Graham-Dixon, Andrew. "Worlds Apart." *The Independent* (London), Nov. 12, 1991, p. 16.

Haus, Mary. "Tatsuo Miyajima: Dreaming by Numbers." *ARTnews* (New York), Nov. 1991, pp. 79–80.

1992 Lingwood, James. "Keep Changing, Connect with Everything, Continue Forever: Tatsuo Miyajima." *Frieze* (London), Mar./Apr. 1992, pp. 18–21.

Renton, Andrew. "Tatsuo Miyajima: Counter Culture." *Flash Art* (Milan), Mar./Apr. 1992, p. 106.

"Added Attraction." *Los Angeles Times*, Jul. 2, 1992, p. F5.

"Insert Tatsuo Miyajima With Piet Mondrian." *Parkett* (Zurich), Dec. 1992, pp. 130–41.

McQuaid, Cate. "Living sculpture fills the ICA. Getting into the Act. 'Performing Objects' makes you part of the show." *The Boston Phoenix*, Dec. 11, 1992, section 3.

Temin, Christine. "'Performing' art that's accessible." *The Boston Globe*, Dec. 12, 1992, pp. 47, 52.

1994 Lutfy, Carol. "Tatsuo Miyajima." *ARTnews* (New York), Apr. 1995, pp. 148–49.

1995 Riddell, Jennifer L. "Tatsuo Miyajima." *New Art Examiner* (Chicago), Mar. 1995, p. 43.

Wakefield, Neville. "Tatsuo Miyajima." *Artforum* (New York), Mar. 1995, p. 88.

Worsdale, Godfrey. "Tatsuo Miyajima." *Art Monthly* (London), Mar. 1995, pp. 28–29.

Padon, Thomas. "Tatsuo Miyajima." *Sculpture* (Washington, D.C.), May/Jun. 1995, p. 42.

Ziegesar, Peter von. "Tatsuo Miyajima at Luhring Augustine." *Art in America* (New York), May 1995, p. 113.

Photographic Credits
pp. 29, 31, 41, 43, 53, 55/56/57/58: Prudence Cuming
Associates, courtesy Anthony d'Offay Gallery, London;
pp. 3/4, 21/22, 25, 27: courtesy Luhring Augustine, New York;
pp. 16, 17, 19: Tadashi Hirose, courtesy Gallery Takagi, Nagoya;
p. 35: Michael Bodycomb, courtesy Modern Art Museum of
Fort Worth; p. 37: Takashi Ebihara; p. 39: J. L. Losi, courtesy
Fondation Cartier pour l'Art Contemporain, Jouy-en-Josas,
France; p. 47: ©Shigeo Anzai, courtesy Faret Tachikawa;
p. 49: courtesy Ripple Across the Water Executive Committee,
Nagasaki; p. 50–51: Steve White, courtesy Artangel Trust,
London

First published in the United States of America in 1996
by Modern Art Museum of Fort Worth
1309 Montgomery Street, Fort Worth, Texas 76107

Reprinted in 1997 by Modern Art Museum of Fort Worth
for the Hayward Gallery, London

Library of Congress Catalog Card Number 96-77588
ISBN 0-929865-15-4

Hayward Gallery edition
ISBN 1-85332-164-8

Hayward Gallery showing organised by Susan May,
assisted by Elena Lukaszewicz

Catalogue designed and produced by Peter B. Willberg, London
Printed in Italy by Grafiche Milani, Milan

Cover: *133651 (Intersect)*, 1990.
L.E.D., IC, electric wire, aluminum panel.
Installation, 223 × 270 1/2 inches. Gallery Takagi, Nagoya.
Frontispiece: *Running Time No. 2*, 1994.
L.E.D., IC, motor, battery.
Individual U-car, 7 1/2 × 4 3/4 × 3 1/2 inches.
Luhring Augustine Gallery, New York.